SOFTWARE DEVELOPMENT

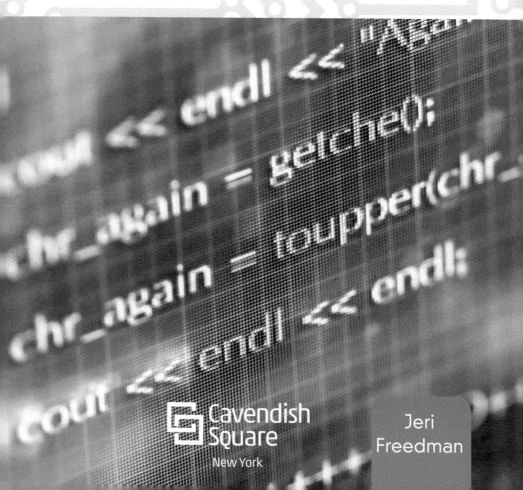

Cavendish
Square
New York

Jeri
Freedman

Published in 2015 by Cavendish Square Publishing, LLC
243 5th Avenue, Suite 136, New York, NY 10016

First Edition

Website: cavendishsq.com

This publication represents the opinions and views of the author based on his or her personal experience, knowledge, and research. The information in this book serves as a general guide only. The author and publisher have used their best efforts in preparing this book and disclaim liability rising directly or indirectly from the use and application of this book.

CPSIA Compliance Information: Batch #WW15CSQ

All websites were available and accurate when this book was sent to press.

Library of Congress Cataloging-in-Publication Data

Freedman, Jeri, author.
Software development / Jeri Freedman.
pages cm. — (High-tech jobs)
Includes bibliographical references and index.
ISBN 978-1-50260-105-6 (hardcover) ISBN 978-1-50260-112-4 (ebook)
1. Computer software—Development—Vocational guidance—Juvenile literature. 2. Computer software industry—Vocational guidance. 3. Computer software developers—Juvenile literature. I. Title.

QA76.76.D47F737 2015
005.1'2023—dc23

2014029733

Editor: Kristen Susienka
Copy Editor: Cynthia Roby
Art Director: Jeffrey Talbot
Senior Designer: Amy Greenan
Senior Production Manager: Jennifer Ryder-Talbot
Production Editor: David McNamara
Photo Researcher: J8 Media

The photographs in this book are used by permission and through the courtesy of: Cover photo and throughout, Trifonenko Ivan. Orsk/Shutterstock.com; Cover photo and 1, wongwean/Shutterstock.com; Moon Light PhotoStudio/Shutterstock.com, 4; ndoeljindoel/Shutterstock.com; 6; ContentWorks/iStock, 8; Odua Images/ Shutterstock.com, 9; UmbertoPantalone/Thinkstock, 10; Rozilynn Mitchell/Shutterstock.com, 12; Time & Life Pictures/the LIFE Images Collection/Getty Images, 13; sspopov/Shutterstock.com, 14; Rob Monk/Edge Magazine/Getty Images, 16; Franck Boston/Shutterstock.com, 21; padu_foto, Shutterstock.com, 23; Anne McQuary/Bloombery/Getty Images, 24–25; Gerber86/iStock, 28; NICHOLAS KAMM/AFP/Getty Images/31; bikeriderlondon/Shutterstock.com 33; Monkey Business Images/Shutterstock.com, 35; Goodluz/Thinkstock, 37; e X p o s e/Shutterstock.com, 39; Alfred Edward Chalon/Science & Society Picture Library/File:Ada Lovelace portrait.jpg/Wikimedia Commons, 40; Justin Sullivan/Getty Images, 41; David Ramos/Getty Images, 42; THOMAS SAMSON/AFP/Getty Images, 44; Andresr/Shutterstock.com, 47; turtix/Shutterstock.com, 48; Vucicevic Milos/Shutterstock.com, 51; moodboard/Thinkstock, 55; sellingpix/Shutterstock.com, 57; auremar/ Shutterstock.com, 61; Daniel Acker/Bloomberg/Getty Images, 63; Peopleimages/Getty Images, 66; Maskot/ Getty Images, 68; Andrew Burton/Getty Images, 71; monkeybusinessimages/Thinkstock, 73; Peopleimages/Getty Images, 76; Dean Drobot/Shutterstock.com, 77; monkeybusinessimages/Thinkstock, 78.

Printed in the United States of America

CONTENTS

Being a software developer lets you create the applications of the future.

INTRODUCTION TO SOFTWARE DEVELOPMENT

Some of the most exciting opportunities today are in software development. The development of smartphones, tablet computers, and the "**cloud**" (remote storage of computer applications and data) has created a boom in the software development field. There is an **insatiable** need for software developers to create every type of application, from games to industrial applications. The Internet and "**app stores**" for Apple and Google Android products have created access to consumers for young developers. The opportunity to promote one's applications has never been greater. Software developers today have the opportunity not only to create new types of software but also to program cutting-edge devices.

The major responsibility of a software developer is the designing of computer programs. That is not the only activity they perform, however. They also test and debug software.

Today, industrial workers use computerized machines to carry out manufacturing tasks.

Since platforms and technologies change frequently, software developers must modify existing programs to incorporate new features or run on different devices. Software developers are sometimes called software engineers.

The Association of Computing Machinery (ACM) is a major organization in the computer industry. It defines software engineering as "the area of study that emphasizes the application of computer languages to developing programs to run computerized applications and managing large software development projects." Examples from the ACM include developing software to run "**avionics**, health-care applications, **cryptography**, traffic control, **meteorological** systems and the like."

Software developers work in some of the fastest-growing and interesting areas of technology. Beyond the experience of being on the cutting edge of computer science, software development as a career offers excellent prospects for employment and job security. Although the U.S. economy is slowly on the upswing after the 2008 economic crisis, landing well-paying and secure jobs, for many, remains a difficult task. One element that contributes to this is the use of high-tech and automated equipment to replace workers performing manual labor. For example, there are many jobs available in the shale oil fields of South Dakota and Texas. However, the work in oil fields that once demanded a worker with a strong back and arms now requires the ability to run sophisticated computerized equipment. The production of many goods in factories is carried out by industrial robots and computerized manufacturing systems.

Administrative positions are also on the decline. When planning vacations, transportation and hotels can be booked through websites. This has eliminated several travel agency positions as well as those of hotel staff. In fact, one person can now perform the duties of managing and running a hotel. A computer with access to savvy hotel management software can control all functions of a hotel and allocate when and where guests will arrive.

To keep pace with consumer demand and a society that thrives on convenience, every industry and business imaginable today needs software developers, and the demand is not likely to end any time soon. Available work will eventually shift to new jobs that technology creates.

Another trend that is increasing the demand for software developers is technologies that allow users to create and upload their own work. Websites such as YouTube have made it possible for people to create and share their own video productions. App and Play stores allow individuals to create and sell programs directly to users. Perhaps you've sold one of your creations there. Social media such as Facebook and Twitter have created new ways of communicating and demonstrate the demand for over-the-Internet software applications. Today, anyone can develop a software application or game and share it with others. This wide availability of access to potential users has made it possible

Some software developers choose to work in startup companies, creating new products and applications.

for anyone to develop a software application and have it widely adopted by users.

The type of software development job you choose depends on both the type of industry you are interested in and the type of software you desire to create. Applications developers develop app software. People think of applications as games and utilities that run on a cell phone. However, applications include very large and complicated suites of office productivity products and scientific software. As an applications developer, you may work alone, with a small group of developers, or as a member of a large team. In the latter case, you may work on one standalone component, or module, of a larger program.

You can also create software to develop and run apps. This area includes developing new operating systems and computer languages. Another area of software development is embedded systems. What makes a digital camera, TV, game console, or multimillion-dollar medical device operate? Computer chips contain the instructions that control the functions of these and thousands of other devices. When a new device is invented, it's up to the software developer to create the instructions that make the device a success.

Some software developer jobs are simply titled "software developer." However, there are some other terms used in the field, including software simulation developer, software engineer, web software developer, software tool developer, and software developer in quality assurance. All of these jobs require slightly different skills and follow a different day-to-day experience. Regardless of the field and type of development you choose, software development provides an exciting opportunity to design the technology not only of the present but also of the future.

You might be wondering whether a career in software development is for you. As you have read, there are many opportunities for software developers today. Maybe you've already written your own software or computer program, or created an app and have sold it online. If so, you're on the right track! This book aims to help you decide on a career path, and determine whether software development is where you should be. It gives you all the information you need to understand what software development is and how you can get involved in the field. Read on to find out more!

Software developers create software for all aspects of a website: the user interface, advertising, payment processing, networking, and more.

Software developers must be able to create applications that run on many different devices, such as tablets, PCs, and smartphones.

1 A CAREER IN SOFTWARE DEVELOPMENT

S oftware development is the creation of computer programs that make electronic devices work and also the applications that run on them. The exact definition of "software developer" varies.

In large and some medium-sized companies a software developer may be responsible for designing software, or supervising lower-level computer programmers who do the actual coding. In smaller companies a software developer may design, code, and test software.

Software developers write applications by using computer languages. Each language uses a set of standard terms to create programs that control the behavior of a standalone computer or a computer incorporated into an electronic device, such as a tablet or smartphone.

At one time, software development consisted of writing programs for computers. Some of these computers were large, such as **mainframes** and even **supercomputers**. Other computers were small like desktop PCs. However, they were all computers. Today, computing capability has been incorporated into a variety of other devices including smartphones, **GPS devices**, iPods, appliances, glasses, and watches. Computer programs run a wide variety of industrial equipment. This includes robots, both fixed-in-place industrial robots and freestanding ones used in military and exploration applications, as well as military drones, which are driverless aircraft and vehicles. Software runs on servers that power online applications such as shopping carts on **e-commerce** sites. Software makes it possible to store information and applications on computer servers and provide access over the Internet, a concept called "the cloud." Software developers create **digital animation** and game programs. There has never been a time when the demand for software developers has been greater. Many industries and applications require software. In addition, new devices for both consumers and industrial use are being developed at an ever-increasing rate. To understand where the field is and where it is going, it is first necessary to understand how the industry has **evolved**.

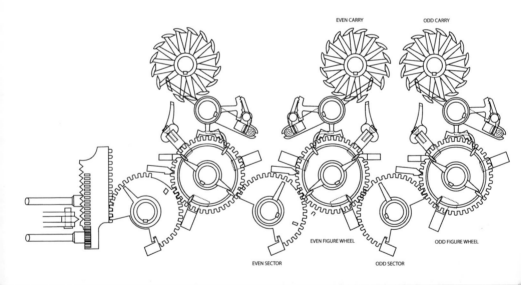

Charles Babbage's "difference engine" used mechanical gears to perform mathematical calculations, automating the process.

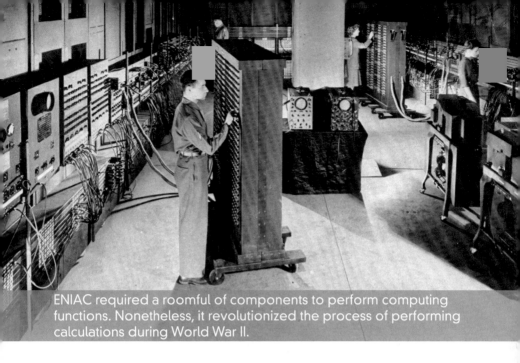

ENIAC required a roomful of components to perform computing functions. Nonetheless, it revolutionized the process of performing calculations during World War II.

THE HISTORY OF SOFTWARE DEVELOPMENT

One of the earliest examples of a programmable device was Charles Babbage's "difference engine," which appeared in the 1800s. This was a "computing" machine designed to perform mathematical calculations and produce tables of results. The difference engine was the first automated calculating machine. The instructions that ran the machine were the earliest example of "software."

World War II fueled the development of the first real computers in the 1940s. Among these early computers was ENIAC (Electronic Numerical Integrator and Computer), developed by J. Presper Eckert and John Mauchly. The goal in designing ENIAC was to automatically calculate firing tables for military use. It was the first electronic computer. Similarly the Harvard-IBM Mark I computer, developed by Howard Aiken, was designed to perform calculations for the U.S. Navy. **Punch cards**, or pieces of cardboard into which holes had been punched, provided the instructions for these early computers.

Microscopic components are applied to a silicon disc. The disc will be cut into numerous tiny silicon chips for use in computers.

Computers first became available for private company use in the 1950s. These were large computers called "mainframes." They required enormous space and had less processing power than today's smartphones. However, the entry of computing into commercial realms, such as accounting, inventory management, and scientific research, led to major advances in programming languages as well as computer hardware. The means of inputting instructions into a computer advanced from punch cards to large spools of magnetic tape.

The invention of the hard drive made it possible to store information on a computer. This advancement meant every instruction did not have to be input every time an activity was performed. Advances in **semiconductor miniaturization** resulted in smaller computer chips. Semiconductors are pieces of silicon modified to transmit electrical signals. The information to create computer chips is imprinted on a silicon disc, which is cut up to create many computer chips; hence, each is a "chip" of silicon. Smaller chips meant computers became even smaller, bringing us minicomputers, PCs, notebook and tablet computers, and ever-smaller consumer devices.

> ## *It's the only job I can think of where I get to be both an engineer and an artist.*
>
> ANDY HERTZFELD, DESIGNER OF THE ORIGINAL APPLE MACINTOSH SOFTWARE, REFERRING TO PROGRAMMING

Early programmers used languages that provided instructions that told the computer what activity to perform on a very basic level at each step of an activity. These languages, such as Assembly Language, used numbers and symbols that were not readily understood by human beings. This fact meant that programming was limited to experts who thoroughly understood computers. It also meant that even simple applications had to be created with large amounts of code, making the process of programming time-consuming and expensive. Over time, new generations of programming languages were created. One of the earliest was BASIC. This language used more user-friendly terms such as "GoTo line 12," which were easier for human beings to understand. The terms were translated by a process called **"compiling"** into commands the computer could understand. Programmers went on to design languages for specific industries. Among these were Pascal, which was developed for scientific applications, and COBOL and Fortran, which were developed for business applications.

As the use of computers spread and the hunger for applications that could be put on those computers continued

The development of easy-to-use computer languages and programming tools has made it possible for anyone to write a computer program or app.

to grow, the demand for easier-to-use languages increased as well. Software developers needed to create more programs faster to meet the ever-rising demand. The 1960s and 1970s saw the development of many of the types of computer languages we use today. These include languages such as Smalltalk that use terms recognizable to human beings, and object-oriented languages such as C, which take programming languages to the next level. Object-oriented languages allow developers to create objects (such as "dog") that contain characteristics (such as size and color). When a programmer writes a program with an object-oriented language, he or she doesn't need to tell the computer about the characteristics of every object referred to because that information is included in each object. This saves programming time and speeds up the process of code development. It also makes it easier to reuse code in another program.

In the 1980s more advanced forms of object-oriented programming languages, such as C++, were developed.

When the Internet and World Wide Web came into general use in the 1990s, languages such as Hypertext Markup Language (HTML) were developed, to make it easier to create web pages. Java and JavaScript were developed to create applications that would run web browsers. Companies began to develop software programs that made it possible to run applications faster and more easily, such as Adobe Flash. In the coming years, software languages and tools will continue to evolve as new devices and applications appear. Those entering the field today will create the new languages that **enhance** the abilities of computerized devices.

WHY DEVELOP SOFTWARE?

Satisfying, challenging, and well-paying jobs for software developers are available today in a wide variety of industries. The need for such expertise is likely to continue. Software developers are in demand in the computer industry itself. A few years ago touch screens and voice-activated computers were nonexistent. One could only enter data via a keyboard or touch pad. Software developers are needed to develop operating systems such as Apple iOS and Windows. They have to create the programs that give computers and other electronic devices the ability to respond to voice commands, react to touchscreen swipes, and otherwise interact with a user. Computer technology is only the beginning of career opportunities for software developers.

Consumer devices are an area of software development today. Companies such as Google, Apple, and Amazon, as well as a large number of smaller companies, are constantly producing improved versions of existing devices. Among these are downloading devices, such as iPads; smartphones, which are capable of browsing the web, providing streaming entertainment, and controlling home electronics remotely; and e-readers and tablet computers. Companies are also working on developing new computing devices. Products under development include **wearables**, devices such as glasses and watches that include web browsing and computing capabilities, and driverless cars, the technology for which is being worked on by companies such as Tesla and Google. Some of these projects will flourish and others may fail, but there is little doubt that it is exciting to work on the technology of the future.

Another advancement is the integration of computers with other types of electronic devices. In other words, there is a progression toward technology that will allow all of your electronic devices to "talk" to each other and exchange information. Your mobile devices, such as tablet computers and smartphones, can now use applications to control lights, locks, and appliances in your house. You can exchange music, photos, data, and video between your tablet computer, smartphone, and home PC, sometimes just by swiping two devices, or passing one over the other. You can upload music from a mobile device to a car stereo system. The mobile revolution of the past few years has resulted in the switch from performing all types of applications on desktop and notebook computers to using smartphones instead. This change has led to a demand for software developers to create new versions of old applications, from games to word-processing software, that will run on smaller devices.

THE SOFTWARE INDUSTRY

It is difficult to nearly impossible to find an industry today that does not rely on computerized systems and equipment. One of the hottest areas for software developers today is entertainment. Computers and the applications that run on them have revolutionized the entertainment industry. Movies have come to rely on computer graphics for many of their special effects, and some consist entirely of computer-generated animation. The computer game industry requires software developers to create their products. The gaming industry has evolved from console games to PC games to mobile games that run on smartphones.

Companies are working to develop virtual reality applications for both games and practical purposes. Digital technology has made it possible for anyone to create and distribute music and video. Companies large and small are working on an ever-increasing number of applications that allow people to upload, modify, and share the music, photos, and videos they create.

Finance may not seem like the most exciting field in which a software developer can work. The term brings to mind accounting and payroll systems. However, software programs have been revolutionizing the way that business is conducted on Wall Street. Where once human analysts pored over company reports to figure out what to buy and sell, now advanced computer programs tell traders what stocks to buy and sell. These programs take a wide variety of factors into consideration, ranging from recent price performance to events in the daily news. In some cases, computers even execute trades automatically. New programs are being developed all the time. This is an exciting area for those interested in economics, mathematics, or the stock market. In companies, software analyzes masses of customer information in **data-mining** applications. **Customer relationship management system (CRM)** software helps sales and marketing maximize their efforts, and **enterprise resource planning (ERP)** software assists production departments in producing goods more efficiently.

Robotics have changed the way that many tasks are done in the twenty-first century and have depended on software developers to program them. Robots range from machines on industrial production lines to independent devices that move and explore environments. Industrial companies are working on larger and more sophisticated machines that can work on their own. Robots are also heavily involved in military and exploratory work. In defense, robots search for mines, and an ever-increasing number of unmanned ground and air vehicles perform surveillance and other activities, reducing the risk to human soldiers. Robots explore caves on Earth and the surface of Mars. In the *BusinessWeek* article "Robots: The Future of the Oil Industry," David Welhe says, "Engineers foresee a day when fully automated rigs roll onto a job site using satellite coordinates, erect 14-story-tall steel reinforcements on their own, drill a well, then pack up and move to the next site." He quotes Professor Eric van Oort, a former Royal Dutch Shell executive, who leads the graduate-level engineering program focused on automated drilling at the University of Texas at Austin. According to van Oort, "You're seeing a new track in the industry emerging. This is going to blossom." Every year, robots of all sorts will continue to be developed, and software developers will be tasked to create programs that animate them.

In the field of health care, software developers create programs for computers that are used in every aspect of medicine. Tablet computers have made it possible for doctors to look up and share information at a patient's bedside. Computerized devices are continuously being developed for testing and monitoring patients remotely. Companies such as Apple, among others, employ software developers who write applications, often called "apps," that allow people to keep track of information such as their heart rate and check their vital signs while exercising, apps some companies hope to incorporate into wearable devices.

Many types of surgery are also being performed using robotic computerized surgical systems controlled by a doctor. Such systems operate with smaller incisions. This type of "minimally" invasive surgery results in less trauma to the patient and faster, less painful recovery. Software developers are needed to create "**knowledge bases**" in a variety of industries. Knowledge bases are very large **databases** containing the knowledge of experts in a particular industry, such as medicine or tech support. Medical professionals can consult the knowledge base to find what diseases are associated with a particular set of symptoms and the recommended treatment.

Data mining is another database application. In data mining, large databases of information are created, and users

Facial recognition software compares a number of points on a person's face with photos in a database to identify a person for security and law enforcement purposes.

IDENTITY PROTECTION

Name:

Password:

00000 000 0 00000000 00100111
0000 0 0000 0 0 0 00 100010111

010011000010 01000111000110
0010111010100011110101010
1101000010 10 11111000

can query (ask questions of) the database, which produces reports showing relationships in the data. For example, a retailer can find out which types of products customers purchase together, or discover the characteristics of customers who purchase particular types of products.

Security is unquestionably a concern in every aspect of life today. People need to protect their homes, personal possessions, and their identity. Similarly, companies need to protect the data on their computer systems. The government and all levels of law enforcement need to protect the public from the attacks of criminals and terrorists. Every level of security relies on computers and requires software developers to create programs to run those systems and to identify possible threats. Software developers write software used to identify suspects, from facial recognition to fingerprint analysis. They develop software for security that uses a person's physical characteristics to control entry to facilities, such as retinal and palm scans. They develop software for new devices used to detect concealed weapons or bombs. Federal agencies such as the Central Intelligence Agency (CIA), the Federal Bureau of Investigation (FBI), and the National Security Agency (NSA) employ software developers to allow them to better analyze and identify terrorist threats before dangerous events occur.

Women in Software Development

One of the problems facing experts in the software development industry is how to get more girls interested in it. According to Sohan Murthy's 2014 article, "Women in Software Engineering: The Dismal Stats," major business networking site LinkedIn examined data worldwide and found that in high-tech software companies only 16 percent of software engineers were female, while in computer hardware companies the percentage of female software engineers was a dismal 9 percent.

Murthy suggests a couple of reasons for the lack of women in software development. First, in the United States, both men and women are taught that women are more valuable if they are attractive, often to the exclusion of other characteristics. This often conflicts with the view women as well as men have of those in STEM (science, technology, engineering, and math) fields as "nerds and geeks." A second problem is that science and technology are hard, for everyone. However, men are more likely to be raised to believe that they are strong and can cope. Boys who are struggling with courses in math and science are more likely to find support from the teacher and encouragement that they can master the material. The attitude toward girls is more likely to be, "Well, girls aren't good at math and science."

Women are also more likely than men to doubt or blame themselves when something goes wrong, and assume they're

Women have just as much ability to succeed as software developers as men, and they will need to participate in the field to fill all the development needs in the future.

not good enough—another culturally absorbed attitude. The issue of attitude is a major problem, and this cultural message begins when girls are in middle or high school, not college. This is bad news because it is very difficult to overcome beliefs and attitudes learned in childhood, when one is most impressionable. In order to have women software developers to recruit, companies are going to have to pressure schools to start interesting girls in technology while they are students and encouraging them to believe they can succeed and master the necessary skills.

TYPES OF SOFTWARE

Software developers work on different types of programs, one of which is the operating system. Operating systems run the functions of a computer and provide users with the ability to access the computer in various ways. General use operating systems include Apple iOS, Windows, and UNIX and its open software version, Linux, among others. Many software developers' jobs involve creating applications. Applications are complete software programs that allow users to perform an activity. The games you download and play on a mobile phone are apps, but apps go far beyond that. Some applications are very large programs that automate a factory. Others run particular devices such as an exploration drone. Others provide users with the ability to obtain online help in operating their new electronic toy, read an electronic book, run a driverless car, or analyze their stock portfolio. Nowadays, developers often have to create different versions of the same app, one to run on desktop, notebook, and tablet computers, and another to run on mobile devices such as smartphones.

WHERE DO SOFTWARE DEVELOPERS WORK?

Obviously, there are many different types of software development jobs, and which type you choose will, to some extent, depend on your personality and interests. If, for example, you have an interest in art or media, entertainment and computer graphics jobs may be of interest. If you excel at math, the financial and business fields can provide **lucrative** positions. If you have an interest in health care, that would be your industry of choice, and so on. In addition to the choice of industry, there is the

Software is often created by a team of developers, each working on a different aspect of the software.

question of what size of company in which you feel comfortable working. The work environment and atmosphere can have a large effect on whether or not you are happy in your career. Companies of all sizes need software developers. There are advantages and disadvantages to working in different-sized companies.

Large corporations offer good salaries and excellent benefits, such as tuition reimbursement, health insurance, and matching funds for 401(k) retirement programs, among other perks. However, large corporations often have more bureaucracy than smaller companies. There are more levels of management and formal processes for obtaining sign-offs on projects and equipment. Small companies, especially startups or those only in business a few years, may provide a more informal atmosphere and an air of excitement if the company is developing a new product or type of application. Dress codes are often more relaxed at a small company. In some cases, the company may also offer stock or stock options to employees, which could become valuable if the company is successful. However, pay may be lower at a small company, and there may be fewer benefits. Also, if the company is developing a new application or technology, the hours may be very long.

Another alternative is to be self-employed. Often this option is a better one after you have gained some experience in a company. However, it can be both lucrative and rewarding. One approach is to develop a standalone application and sell it either through existing resources, such as Apple's App Store, or to a corporation. Another approach is to provide custom software development services directly to companies. In this case the developer is hired to create or modify a computer program used by a company for a specific business purpose, such as accounting, customer tracking, or product management. Some of the advantages of being self-employed are that you're responsible only to yourself and the customers, you can schedule your own time to work, and get to keep all the money you make after expenses and taxes. The disadvantages are that there is no job security. You must continue to search for work; provide your own insurance; do all the sales, advertising, and marketing necessary to attract customers; and you may be constantly on call in case a customer experiences a problem. If you're interested in self-employment, one approach is to work on developing an app while still in school or college. This was done, for example, by Facebook founder Mark Zuckerberg, who developed the early version of Facebook while a student at Harvard.

Corporate culture is defined as the "general atmosphere" of a company. This is influenced by many factors that are not strictly related to the company's size. One element of corporate culture is how formally or informally a company's environment is structured. A company may offer its employees hot and cold snacks and skateboard ramps in the parking lot. Or it may be a consulting firm where everyone wears a suit and tie. Many small companies are very informal. However, even large companies such as Google may try to foster an attitude of informality, in the belief that this type of environment inspires creativity. Other companies have a more formal corporate atmosphere. Do you like creative chaos or calm and order? All these elements must be taken into account when considering where you want to work as a software developer.

CAREER PATHS FOR SOFTWARE DEVELOPERS

Typically, a person will start out as a software developer or software engineer, or sometimes as a junior software developer, eventually advancing to senior software developer or engineer. The software developer spends most of his or her time coding software. Those in this position may also be responsible for testing software to make sure that it operates properly and finding and fixing **bugs** (program errors). Senior software developers sometimes become team leaders, called "lead software developers." Those in this position may have responsibility for overseeing the progress of the project, ensuring that it stays on time and on track. Those who manage the development of a software project are sometimes called "software development project managers." Project managers are responsible for assigning people and physical resources, tracking the progress of a project, and resolving conflicts. They must also work with users to establish their requirements and make sure the components of the software being developed meets those needs.

The software development manager oversees the software development department. The team leaders report to the manager on the progress of their projects. The manager is not usually involved in the hands-on coding of software. Instead, he or she is responsible for high-level supervision. The manager's duties include budgeting, allocating resources, tracking progress of multiple projects, and reporting on the status of these projects to senior management of the company.

Now that you know what a software developer is, you might wonder what skills and education you need to become one. That's where we begin in Chapter 2.

Because many people work together on a project, interpersonal skills are important to succeeding as a software developer.

2 BECOMING A SOFTWARE DEVELOPER

Software developers require two types of skills, technical and personal. Technical skills are usually learned in college classes, which most people in the industry pursue after high school. Personal skills are developed through interacting with others. Both are important to have when considering software development as a career. This chapter will examine what skills are needed and what type of education you should receive to get the best job possible in software development.

CREATING CODE AND SOFTWARE

To create computer programs and apps, a software developer writes computer code, which tells the computer what to do. A variety of languages exist that a software developer can use to write programs. Which language a developer uses depends on the type of program and the operating system on which it runs.

Some of the most popular programming languages are **C**, **C++**, **C#**, Java, and Visual Basic. Students are not expected to enter college knowing how to write software in specific languages, but they are expected to have the academic knowledge to learn how to do so. To program well, software developers need a solid knowledge of logic and math.

Creating software that runs on a company's own internal systems is different from creating an app used by thousands, or even millions, of people around the globe. Creating an app is different from creating software to control the functions of an automobile or robot. Specific computer languages are better suited to particular applications. There is no guarantee exactly what type of job a software developer will get. Therefore, it's common for software developers to learn many different programming languages while in college. That is not the end for software developers, however. New languages and new devices are being developed all the time. Software developers must be prepared to continue adding to their repertoire of languages over the course of their career. For this reason, the willingness and ability to learn independently is one of the skills employers value most highly.

THE VALUE OF INTERPERSONAL SKILLS

Matt Weisfeld, associate professor at Cuyahoga Community College in Cleveland, Ohio, conducted a study on the skills employers most value in a potential software developer. During the study, Weisfeld interviewed employers in small, medium, and large companies. Although you might expect that employers' major emphasis would be on a good knowledge of programming languages, the study revealed that the skill most desired by employers is the ability to learn. Employers expect developers to understand the fundamentals of logic and programming, but they want developers who can learn languages they don't already know and move from one language to another. While many students concentrate heavily on developing their technical skills, interpersonal skills often turn out to be critical to succeeding in the field as well. Across the board, employers want software developers with a combination of both technical and "soft" skills, such as communication and presentation skills. These also include interpersonal skills. Except for very small apps, it's rare today for a program to be developed by a single software developer. Those in this field must be able to work well as members of a team and get along with others. Software developers also need to have a creative vision. They need to see the possibilities for new approaches and applications.

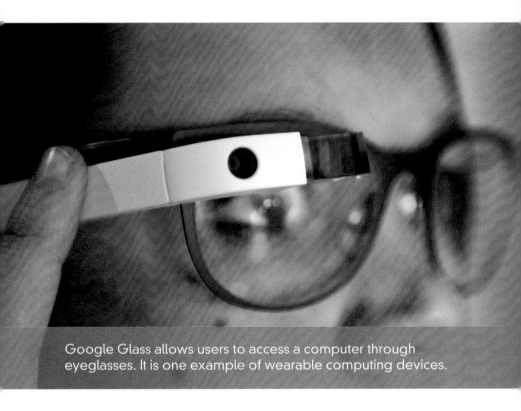

Google Glass allows users to access a computer through eyeglasses. It is one example of wearable computing devices.

Another skill most highly valued by employers is the ability to solve problems. Software development is full of issues that arise when creating software. Bugs are constantly encountered and are often hard to **isolate**. Software programs must run on multiple platforms, or operating systems. Developers often must create different versions of the software for different operating systems. Software must function on desktop computers with large amounts of memory and processing power and also run on tiny mobile devices. Software must be integrated to work with existing programs and hardware, and it must constantly be modified to operate on new versions of existing operating systems. It must sometimes operate remotely in the cloud. It must be modified to work new devices and technologies as they arise, and altered as the customer's or end user's needs change. Every time a program is changed, new problems arise, and a large part of a software developer's job is to deal with and solve problems.

LAYING THE FOUNDATION

If you decide to pursue a career in software development, the time to start preparing is while you are in middle or high school. That is the best time to establish the foundation that will allow you to develop specific skills that will make you successful in college and on the job.

Some schools offer courses in computers, and more have computer clubs where students practice writing software programs. If these options are available at your school, take advantage of them. Trying out software coding firsthand is the surest way to see if such a career will interest you. In addition to receiving hands-on experience in programming, you will gain knowledge of the types of problems and solutions you will encounter in the real world. Creating a cool application can be very satisfying, but doing so requires patience and hours of hard work.

Most companies today prefer software developers to have a college degree. This guarantees that they have the fundamentals to successfully learn and use today's sophisticated programming languages and tools. Computer science and software development curricula contain a large number of math and science courses. To be prepared for these courses in college, you need to get a solid grounding in those subjects in middle and high school.

Math is the basis for computer code. Therefore, learning mathematics provides the foundation for a software development career.

Specific classes you should look into taking in high school include math classes, such as:

- Algebra
- Pre-calculus
- Calculus (the branch of mathematics that forms the basis of computer algorithms (steps for performing a task))
- Statistics
- Physics

However, the most important things you can learn in high school are basic skills that can be applied to a variety of situations and are critical to being successful. As you have already read, employers want employees who can communicate effectively both verbally and in writing. Software developers must be able to communicate with other software developers, managers, customers, and end users. That means you must be able to organize your ideas well and speak and write in a way that is clear and understandable to those who do not have your knowledge of programming. To communicate well, you need to have a solid knowledge of English grammar and syntax.

Take whatever opportunities are offered to practice your writing skills. Practicing public speaking skills is beneficial as well. During the course of your career, you will most likely find yourself making presentations—to potential customers and to management. So, if your school offers a public speaking course, it's a good idea to take it. There is no way to get around the fact that software developers spend a great deal of time at the keyboard, so if your school provides a typing or keyboarding course, taking it could enhance your coding by making it faster and more efficient.

HONING YOUR SKILLS IN OTHER WAYS

The more experience and understanding you have of computers and software, the better prepared you will be for a career. You can do this by volunteering to work in your school's computer lab, if it has one; helping a charitable organization, such as your local Boys and Girls Club or teen center, with their computers or tutoring children there on how to use them; and practicing making apps yourself. Companies such as Apple offer beginners' app-development kits.

Online resources are also useful to learning about the software development industry. Listed here are a few websites specializing in software development resources:

- **CoderDojo** (coderdojo.com) matches up young people with volunteer mentors to provide training in coding.

- **Dream in Code** (dreamincode.net/forums/showforum78. htm) is a portal, meaning a site with links to other websites, to online tutorials for a variety of popular software languages, including specific languages,

Teaching kids about computers can be a great way to hone your own skills—and it can be fun!

game design, cloud computing, mobile software development, and others.

- **GirlDevelopIt** provides classes and resources for girls, with chapters around the country. For more information go to girldevelopit.com.

- **Girls Who Code** (girlswhocode.com) is a national nonprofit group that provides training and resources to girls ages thirteen to seventeen who are interested in learning to code.

- **Internet4Classrooms** (internet4classrooms.com/on-line. htm) provides tutorials for students on web development software including Dreamweaver and Java, computer operating systems, and other computer-related topics.

- **Clubhouses** are organizations, such as the Intel Computer Clubhouse Network, that provide locations around the country and the world where youth from low-income households can learn computer skills. A list of clubhouses is available at: computerclubhouse.org.

Using these and similar resources allows you to see if you enjoy programming, and to obtain some advance preparation for college courses if you do.

If you are serious about a programming career and enjoy creating apps, it's possible to practice programming skills by creating apps that you can share with friends, post on a social networking site such as Facebook, or even offer through a site that sells apps, such as Apple's App Store or Google's Play Store. If your app becomes successful in these online stores, it could provide you with spending money and give you a great résumé item.

EDUCATION FOR SOFTWARE DEVELOPMENT

Most software developer jobs require a four-year college degree. Although experienced programmers may be hired without one, the environment is more competitive for those just starting out. As a student getting a degree in software development, you will study both hardware and software. This is important because software developers need to understand how the hardware works in order to know how to program it. In addition, they must know the general principles that govern how electronic devices work. This knowledge allows them to understand new electronic devices as they appear. In addition to learning about hardware and computer languages, students learn how to effectively approach projects and solve problems. This knowledge is critical when one is designing software for a project.

It is unlikely that you will be put in charge of a large project if you get a software development job right out of college. Most likely you will start out as a member of a team, responsible for one part of a project. The higher a person advances in a software development career, the broader the base of knowledge employers demand. Many colleges offer bachelor's degree programs as well as

In college, students can study advanced programming applications such as robotics, artificial intelligence, and new technologies being developed for the next generation of devices.

master's degree and Ph.D. programs. Those interested in working in cutting-edge technologies and programming, including areas such as **artificial intelligence** and advanced robotics, and those planning to do research into new technologies, may wish to pursue higher-level degrees.

It is possible in some cases to enter the field as a junior-level programmer without a four-year bachelor's degree, especially in smaller companies. Those in this position start out doing basic computer programming tasks. A two-year associate's degree and hands-on experience may be sufficient. Advancing to higher-level jobs, especially at a different company, may be easier with a four-year degree. However, it is possible to complete a four-year degree while working, and many companies offer tuition reimbursement programs. These programs reimburse employees for successfully completing courses related to their job.

This approach can significantly reduce the cost of college. Most bachelor's degree programs give credit for courses taken for the associate's degree. Technical institutes offer both four-year degree programs and two-year associate's degree programs. Associate's degree programs concentrate on particular technical skills related to software development and programming, such as software applications development, while bachelor's degrees offer a more diverse educational background.

Another option is to study for a degree online. Software development is the type of activity that lends itself to this approach because programming can be done easily at home, and practical skills are more important in many cases than where a person got his or her degree. However, one must have a great deal of self-discipline to do the work without the support system available at a physical college. If you decide to pursue a degree online, it is necessary to ensure that the institution offering the program is accredited just like a physical college. Therefore, you should check the U.S. Department of Education database of accredited colleges, where colleges can be looked up by name. Getting a degree from an accredited school ensures the program is valid and one can obtain a valid degree or transfer credits to another school if necessary.

SOFTWARE DEVELOPMENT CURRICULUM

Which college-level courses students take depends to some degree on what type of development they want to do and the type of industry in which they are interested in working. However, the following information provides a general look at the types of courses a student takes when learning software development.

Students will take general courses in computer science, mathematics, and natural sciences, as well as courses in several areas of computer science. General courses on the subject can be applied to any field in which students decide to work. A few examples of such courses include Introduction to Computer Systems, Introduction to Data Structures, programming courses in specific languages such as C and Unix, and **computational** mathematics. Students will also take courses in specific areas of computer science that interest them. Examples include multimedia, robotics, computer graphics, game design, and artificial intelligence. As mentioned earlier, students will most likely take many mathematics courses. They can also expect to take courses in the natural sciences, such as physics, and basic courses in engineering and experimental design. The latter is considered key to being able to design a technology project.

A typical college curriculum in software development will include courses in mathematics that apply to computer programming, such as linear algebra, calculus, and statistics. It will include courses in specific computer languages. If the emphasis is on programming, it may cover various popular software development applications. If the emphasis is on software design

A page of computer code onscreen. Part of students' software development education is the hands-on creation of lots of computer code.

and engineering, it may include courses in project management and quality assurance. Students may also be required to take a course in ethics, which may include ethical computing, particularly how to maintain the confidentiality of data and protect people's privacy. Students will most likely do work in a computer lab, where they will

Who's Who in Software Development

There are many people who have contributed to the field of software development. The following is a list of a few of the industry's major contributors.

Ada Lovelace was the daughter of the poet Lord Byron. She was the first programmer. She created the computer algorithm that ran Charles Babbage's "analytical engine," which was designed in the 1840s.

Bill Gates, along with his business partner, Paul Allen, founded Microsoft Corporation, the largest software company in the world. Microsoft was seminal in developing software to run on personal computers, from operating systems to office applications and games. Gates retired from Microsoft in 2008.

This portrait shows Ada Lovelace, who wrote the first computer program in the nineteenth century.

Steve Jobs, cofounder of Apple Computer, was responsible for pioneering many computer devices, from the icon-based user interface for computers to the smartphone.

Steve Jobs cofounded Apple Inc. with Steve Wozniak. The company revolutionized the way users interacted with computers by producing the first icon-based software. This software allowed users to access the functions of a computer simply by clicking on the screen. Prior to that, users had to type in every command, even simple ones, on a keyboard. He continued to be a driving force at the company, producing such innovative products as the iPod, iPhone, and iPad, until his death in 2011.

Larry Ellison and his partners, Robert Miner and Ed Oates, founded Oracle Corporation. They pioneered the use of structured query language (SQL) to create the database system Oracle. The company is named after their first project, developing an advanced database for the CIA, codenamed Oracle.

Tim Berners-Lee invented the World Wide Web, the web page technology that allows us all to share information over the Internet. Berners-Lee was at the European Particle Physics Laboratory (CERN) in Switzerland at the time. He created the first web client and server software in 1990 and wrote the initial specifications for Universal Resource Locators (web addresses), Hypertext Markup Language (the language used to create web pages), and the Hypertext Transport Protocol (HTTP) to transmit information over the Internet.

Linus Torvalds is the creator of Linux, the open software version of the UNIX operating system. Linux is a major operating system used by organizations worldwide. His approach to operating system development was revolutionary at the time. He made the source code available to anyone who wanted to use it, and allowed it to be modified and redistributed freely by members of the computing community.

Mark Zuckerberg is founder and CEO of the social media company Facebook. He began programming when he was twelve, creating applications and games with his friends. He created the first version of Facebook with friends Dustin Moskovitz, Chris Hughes, and Eduardo Saverin during his sophomore year at Harvard University. In 2014, Facebook had over 1 billion users.

Jack Dorsey began dabbling in web development while in college. He founded the social networking site Twitter in 2006 and served as its first chief executive officer (CEO).

Mark Zuckerberg, chief executive officer of Facebook, the world's largest social networking company.

perform computer-related tasks and write programs. Thus, they will be expected to demonstrate hands-on knowledge of the material the courses cover.

In the workplace, a software developer needs more than technical skills to succeed. A software developer needs good communication and managerial skills. Often organizational and people skills are more critical to making a project successful than programming skills. Many college software development curricula require students to take a course on communications for engineers. Even if such a course isn't required, it is highly recommended that you take one if offered by the school. If project management isn't explicitly required but is offered as an elective at the college, it's advisable to take that as well. When getting a bachelor's degree, in addition to technical courses, students will be expected to take a variety of courses in the humanities and arts. Courses such as psychology, the history of other cultures, and languages can be particularly helpful. If you are considering eventually starting your own business or working as a freelance software developer, it's desirable to take some courses in business management, budgeting, and finance.

Above all, when in college, take the opportunity to develop good work habits. Software development is a field in which you will often have to work without supervision, organize your time, complete work in a timely fashion, and produce high-quality work. Developing these habits while in college will increase your chances of being successful on the job.

PAYING FOR YOUR EDUCATION

For many, a college education has become difficult to afford. However, before becoming discouraged, be aware that there are a number of resources that can help you pay for college. Most technical schools and colleges have a financial aid department that helps students apply for financial aid packages. Student loans are one means of covering the cost of college. Since government guidelines regulate student loans, they often have low interest

I was lucky to be involved and get to contribute to something that was important, which is empowering people with software.

BILL GATES,
COFOUNDER OF MICROSOFT

Software Development

rates. However, they must be repaid after graduation, which means giving up some of your income.

There are resources designed specifically to assist low-income students. One such resource is the U.S. Federal Supplemental Education Opportunity Grant, which assists low-income students in paying for college. (For more information go to www2.ed.gov/programs/fseog.) If you are the child of a veteran, it pays to check with the Veterans Administration regarding benefits for which you may be eligible. Children of veterans, as well as veterans themselves, are entitled to certain educational assistance benefits under the G.I. Bill. The G.I. Bill website, at gibill.va.gov, provides more information.

The Institute of Electrical and Electronics Engineers, an electronics industry professional organization, offers a variety of scholarships to its student members. It provides information, and a listing of other sources of scholarships as well, at sites.ieee.org/sb-morgan/member-benefits/scholarships. For a listing of all types of funding available to students from IEEE, visit ieee.org/organizations/foundation/educationalfunds.html.

A number of U.S. government agencies, such as the NSA, CIA, and FBI, also offer scholarships and tuition assistance programs to students in computer science who are willing to work for them after college. For more information see these agencies' websites. The military also offers tuition assistance programs. The military is not a career that is right for everyone. However, if you are interested in serving in the armed forces, most branches of the armed services offer ROTC programs. These programs pay for all or part of a college education in a technical field such as computer science. If you are interested in such a program, you must arrange it at a recruitment center before enlisting and before enrolling in a college.

In addition to funds provided by outside sources, many colleges and universities also offer work-study programs. In this type of program, students work a certain number of hours each week for the college and, in turn, receive payment to help cover their expenses.

CONTINUED LEARNING

Technology constantly changes. New devices and elements that control these devices are invented every year. Therefore, software developers may have to learn new software development techniques and familiarize themselves with new hardware technologies to keep up with current trends. A good way to continue learning is by participating in certificate programs. Certificate programs are designed primarily for working professionals who wish to expand their knowledge of computer science or programming. They generally require one or two years to complete and are often offered part-time.

GET A BROAD EDUCATION

Today business and entertainment are both global activities. Regardless of what type of company you work for, chances are that you will find yourself dealing with users, customers, and staff members from other countries. No matter what type of product you work on, it will most likely end up being sold to or used by people in other countries. You may even have to travel to other countries to work on software projects at other branches of the company that employs you.

Closer to home, you will be working with people from different ethnic and cultural backgrounds. Different cultures have different attitudes toward many behaviors. Understanding and being sensitive to these attitudes and cultural beliefs is important. For that reason, you should not restrict your learning to technical courses. As with most undergraduate degree programs, students in software development bachelor's degree programs must take general courses in liberal arts and the humanities. Take advantage of this opportunity to expand your knowledge of people and cultures. Taking courses in areas such as history, philosophy, and psychology can help in understanding how people interact and their attitudes and behaviors. Showing an understanding of and sensitivity to other people's cultures and

Programming is done by and for a wide range of people. The wider your range of knowledge, the more successful you will be in understanding and satisfying them.

beliefs creates a positive impression on others and makes work go more smoothly.

If you are interested in working in a particular field, such as finance, entertainment, scientific research, or health care, geological or ecological simulation, or aerospace, it can be helpful to take courses in your chosen area in addition to software development courses. Having knowledge of the particular industry in which you want to work can make you more competitive when applying for a job. It will also make your work easier because you will be familiar with the terminology and issues in your chosen field.

Having a broad base of knowledge, encompassing technology, communication, science, business, and humanities, demonstrates to employers that you have the combination of skills to succeed as an employee. Today's employers want employees who are not only proficient in their technical field but have the ability to solve problems and work well with others.

As of 2013, Google employed more than 47,000 people, including 10,000 software developers. It has forty offices around the world.

3 LANDING AND DOING THE JOB

A ccording to a report by market research firm Gartner, worldwide software revenue in 2013 was $403.3 billion. Revenue increased 4.8 percent from 2012. The following list of a few of the world's largest software companies provides some ideas as to the software being used and developed today.

- **Microsoft**, the largest software manufacturer in the world, is headquartered in Redmond, Washington. Founded in 1975, Microsoft is most well known for its Windows operating systems, Internet Explorer web browser, and Microsoft Office suite of applications. It produces the Xbox and has a large computer game division and cloud computing services.

- **Apple Computer** started out in 1976, creating the first Apple PC in a garage, and has become the premiere maker of computerized consumer electronic devices, changing the music industry with the iPod and downloadable music. It changed both the telephone and computer industries with the invention of the iPhone smartphone, and produced the first tablet computer, the iPad. The company continues to work in new areas such as wearables, Apple TV, and other innovative products.

- **Google**, long the number one search engine, creates some of the most innovative software and services. It has created the world's most popular search engine, Chrome, and the successful Android smartphone operating system. It maintains a large research division working on cutting-edge development projects.

- **Facebook** is the largest social media site in the world, with more than 1.2 billion users as of 2014. Facebook employs a large number of software developers. In addition to adding new features and services, it has been actively acquiring other social media companies, such as Instagram, and is likely to continue its growth in exciting ways in the near future.

- **Oracle Corporation** is the largest database software corporation in the world, with more than 400,000 customers worldwide. The company employs 35,000 developers. Its SQL database software runs both at company sites and in the cloud. It is used by customers in 145 countries.

- **IBM**, founded in 1911 as International Business Machines, is one of the oldest companies in the computer field. IBM introduced the first mainframe computer in 1959 and the first desktop PC in 1981. Today IBM primarily provides businesses with software and services, including both enterprise and cloud applications.

- **Symantec Corporation**, founded in 1982, has become the world's largest commercial security software company.

Large companies often purchase small ones that develop new types of software applications, such as Facebook's 2012 purchase of Instagram because of its instant messaging app.

It provides security, storage, and systems management solutions for both consumers and businesses.

- **EMC Corporation**, founded in 1979, provides storage, data protection, data analysis, cloud, and security services to companies worldwide. It is one of the largest storage solutions companies in the world. Its **big data** services are focused on collecting, storing, and analyzing massive amounts of data in real time.

- **Hewlett-Packard (HP)** is the world's largest manufacturer of personal computers. Often thought of as a manufacturer of PCs and printers, its software division is one of the top seven software producers in the world. HP provides business software, mobile applications, service management, security, big data analysis software, and software consulting services.

- **CA Technologies** provides software development, service management, data protection, security, database management, quality assurance, and automation software and services. The company's software runs on platforms ranging from mainframe computers to mobile devices and both on-site and cloud systems. "The advanced research organization within CA Technologies, CA Labs, leverages leading-edge, collaborative research from universities around the world."

- **Salesforce** is the leading provider of customer relationship management (CRM) software. CRM involves identifying, targeting, and providing support to customers. The company provides software to generate sales leads and to manage the customer services process. Salesforce pioneered this field and continues to be the major supplier of computerized sales and customer support software to businesses.

- **Adobe Systems** produces some of the most commonly used software for consumer, professional, and business multimedia use. The company's products include, among others, Photoshop, Illustrator, Flash, and Acrobat. Adobe software has been engineered to run on computers, on mobile devices, and in the cloud.

WORKING AS A SOFTWARE DEVELOPER

What do software developers actually do when they arrive at the office Monday morning? Software developers produce, test, and implement computer codes for applications or products. Software development managers spend much of their time working with programmers writing the code. They also spend time researching and choosing outside resources when necessary. These may include content providers, graphic artists, and others required for a specific project. They oversee the development of the end product—application, packaged software product, or program to run a device—from development through testing and debugging

> ## " "
> *People think that computer science is the art of geniuses but the actual reality is the opposite, just many people doing things that build on each other, like a wall of mini stones.*
>
> DONALD KNUTH, COMPUTER SCIENTIST AND PROFESSOR EMERITUS, STANFORD UNIVERSITY

to final distribution. They spend a significant amount of time coordinating the team members. Software developers work with computer programs such as C, C++, and Java.

Developers can work anywhere from eight to fourteen hours a day, depending on the stage of development of a product and how well development is going. Long hours are most likely when a deadline is approaching, especially for a new product release or for delivery to a customer. Software development is often tracked to see if it is meeting a schedule. If difficulties or bugs are causing a project to be behind schedule, everyone on the team may have to work longer hours to catch up. The unexpected often occurs in software development, especially when working with new devices and technology. Therefore software developers have to be flexible. On one hand, they have to organize their time so that they can complete their part of a project without holding up others, but they also need to be able to adjust to the unexpected.

Because software developers are likely to encounter many issues in getting a program or application to perform as desired, they need to be able to work through problems and deal with frustration. Members of a team must work together if a program is going to be completed successfully. Therefore, software developers must have excellent interpersonal skills. They must be able to communicate progress and issues without antagonizing other team members. They must also be willing to support other members of the team. Working in this field can be very exciting today because there are so many new applications and devices being developed, hence the camaraderie of working to develop something new.

A DAY IN THE LIFE

A typical day in the life of a software developer may be something like the following:

9 a.m. Arrive at work. Check e-mail for any important issues or activities. Check software logs to see if any new bugs or problems have arisen. Arrange schedule for the day and make a to do list.

10 a.m–1 p.m. Work on code for current project. Work may vary according to the phase of the project. It may require writing code, reviewing code, testing code, or fixing bugs.

2–4 p.m. Write more code. Assist with answering support queries from clients using the company's software. Send completed and initially tested code for new feature to quality assurance department for further testing.

4:00 p.m. Attend a team meeting to review who is working on what, what help is required and from whom, any new technologies worth considering, and progress toward completing current projects. Make recommendations regarding proposed architecture and functionality for new project.

5:00 p.m. Check code into code-tracking system. Check e-mail and address anything critical before leaving.

Evening and weekend work: If a product is in release or upgrade phase, a developer may need to work evening or weekend hours to deploy new software. During these hours, the servers it will run on will have low usage. This may also be the case if a deadline is approaching for the launch of a new product.

Being a software developer is not a nine-to-five job. It sometimes requires working long hours to complete a project on schedule.

WHAT'S INVOLVED IN PROGRAMMING?

Computer languages all have a unique syntax, which is the set of rules for how to construct commands. This syntax is like the rules of grammar that govern the construction of sentences. Standard syntax makes the information being communicated clear. This syntax allows programmers to write commands in English that can be translated or compiled into instructions the computer understands. To provide an idea of what is involved in programming, the following list, summarized from Computer Hope (a computer help website), contains some of the elements of syntax that a software developer must understand, regardless of the language used.

- **Variables:** These are elements whose values change when the program is run, such as color or quantity. Software developers must know how to declare variables, or provide a location for the variable.

- **Conditional statements:** These are commands that tell the computer where to go in a program based on a given condition, such as: If "yes" then GoTo line 12. If "no" then GoTo line 13. The format of conditional statements varies from language to language.

- **Loops:** Loops are pieces of code a program performs over and over until another command tells it to stop. For example, a loop is used to count down from ten to zero, subtracting one number from a counter each time until zero is reached.

- **Escape sequences:** An escape sequence is two or more symbols or letters that tell a computer to perform an action or display text. For example, the symbol \" might be used to make the computer show a quotation mark on screen instead of interpreting it as part of the code.

- **Comments:** These are notes the software developer puts in the code to tell other programmers what that piece of code is doing. Each language has a format for comments, which lets the computer know that the line in question is not part of the actual code. For example, in C, /*Test module 1*/ is a comment.

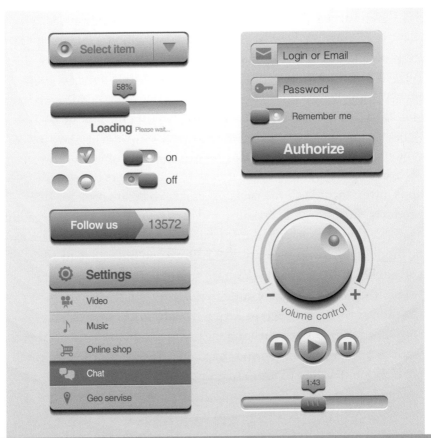

The elements of a software development kit. Such kits allow developers to put standard buttons and other elements in programs without having to create them from scratch.

Writing your own application or game is an excellent way to get a hands-on feel of what it's like to program. What are the steps to create a program? First, you must decide whether your program will run on a PC or tablet computer, a mobile device, or online, perhaps on a site such as Facebook. Next you must decide what language to use for the program. C# is one of the most commonly used languages for the creation of games and apps. You write the actual program in a text editor, commonly referred to as "an editor." You can use an ordinary text-editing program such as Microsoft Notepad or Apple's TextEdit. There are also a variety of programmable text editors, which include special features that make coding easier. Finally, you may need a compiler. A compiler is a program that takes the code written in a language such as Java and turns it into a form the computer can understand. Some languages need compilers and some don't. If the language needs to be compiled, the source from which you obtained information on the language should also have information on compilers used with it.

Software development kits provided by companies such as Microsoft and Apple, to make it easy for developers to create apps, often include all the tools necessary to create code for their products, including a text editor and compiler. These kits are readily available to developers, and information on how to obtain them can be found on the company's website. Once you have all your tools, you should create a simple program to learn the language. It's a tradition to write a piece of code that prints out "Hello, world" to the monitor. You can then experiment with other elements.

Once familiar with the language, you need to decide what you want your program to do, and map out a design for the different parts. Then it's time to jump in and program. Your work is not finished when you're done programming. Once your program is done, you will need to test it, and have others test it too, so you can catch and fix any bugs. Only when the program is debugged as well as possible is the program ready for sharing or uploading.

FINDING A JOB

Once you have decided that you want to pursue a career in software development, and have completed your education, the next step is to find a job. The first thing that most people think of when they consider looking for a job is to check the job classifieds. Most people in the computer industry use online job classifieds. Online job-hunting sites include CareerBuilder.com, Monster. com, and LinkedIn. Since demand for software developers is so great, there are a large number of ads. It's common nowadays for companies and government agencies to list job openings right on their website. If you are interested in working for a particular company or in a particular industry, go to the websites of those companies and click on the "Careers" or "Jobs" link.

However, there is also a lot of competition for jobs because many people view the same ad. So, don't just send résumés to companies that advertise. Jobs are opening up all the time at companies, especially large ones. Often these jobs are filled without ever being advertised. To reduce the time spent searching for a position, you want to get résumés into the hands of a large number of potential employers. The person who receives the résumé may have a job that has not yet been advertised. If not, the recipient may file the résumé so that if a need arises in the future, he or she can contact you. Also, the recipient may not need someone with your skills at the moment, but may pass the résumé along to a colleague who does. You can combine this approach with others to increase your chances of finding a position.

Since such a vast range of industries and manufacturers needs software developers, there is no reason to restrict a job search to only software companies. For instance, industrial companies like General Electric need software developers for their products. You can use an online industry directory or general business directory such as the Standard & Poor's or Dow Jones directories to locate companies that look interesting. These directories can usually be accessed at libraries. Send your résumé to the director of software development or IT department.

The most successful way to find a job is often through networking, the kind that involves people, not computers. When networking, job seekers can contact people they know in the field and ask them for assistance in locating a job. This is where having developed contacts through interning, participating in the open source community and problem-solving forums, and joining industry organizations can help get the word out that you are looking for a job. It's helpful to get the name, e-mail address, and when possible business card of the people encountered in those activities so that you can contact them when job hunting. Even if they don't know of a job opening, they may be able to provide the names of people who might be able to help.

Internships

An internship is an excellent way to experience firsthand what is involved in software development. It also allows students to demonstrate to potential employers that they have the basic skills necessary to perform successfully in the workplace. Internships are unpaid positions at a company. An internship provides the chance to learn and apply real-world skills on the job. Interns assist professionals working on actual projects. Although interns perform basic tasks, they have the opportunity to observe all the aspects of a job they aspire to have. There is no substitute for seeing how the techniques taught in class are used on the job. Perhaps more importantly, internships give interns the chance to learn how professionals deal with problems and people in the workplace.

In addition, if interns perform well, the professionals they work with may be willing to provide a reference when they are applying for a job. In many cases the people the intern works with may remain valuable resources in the future.

Some colleges have a work-study program. In this type of program students spend a semester working as interns at a company as part of their educational program. If your college doesn't offer such a program, or to find a summer opportunity, start your own search by exploring the organizations' websites listed.

- Institute of Electrical and Electronics Engineers (IEEE), ieeeusa.org/careers/student.menu.html
- American Society for Engineering Education (ASEE) Tech Intern, tech-interns.com

An intern checks code. Internships allow one to experience how software development is done in the real world.

Many companies in the software field list internships on their websites in the "Careers" or "Jobs" sections. Some companies even have a dedicated section of the website specifically for college students who are interested in a summer job or internship. Some software companies will hire students while they are completing their final year of college, so be sure to check out the websites of individual companies to see what opportunities are available.

Most colleges and technical schools have a placement office, or Career Services center. This office assists students with their job search. The placement office often provides additional services such as resources for writing résumés and other job-hunting tools. Often educational institutions host job fairs. Companies participating in the job fair send representatives to the campus to discuss jobs. Job fairs provide a chance to get an idea of what companies are doing. Even if they are not specifically looking for software developers, often the representatives can provide information on whom to contact about such work. For the same reason, if a computer industry organization is hosting a conference or tradeshow in or nearby your area, it is worth talking to the company representatives at the show to find out what person or department to contact about potential jobs. The IEEE and ACM provide career-seeking information for their members, including newsletters that list job opportunities and web pages with job search utilities. As you approach graduation, these sites can also be valuable resources.

Because software developers are in high demand, recruitment agencies (or headhunters) are often asked to locate candidates to fill these jobs. You can search for recruitment agencies in your area online or in your local phone book. You can send your résumé to a recruitment agency the same way you do to a potential employer. Recruitment agencies are most useful when you have specialized training, are highly experienced, or are applying for a high-level position. When a recruitment agency has a position they think would be suitable, they will contact you with the details. Be sure that your level of experience and training makes you a good candidate for the particular job. There have been instances when recruitment agencies were simply trying to parade a large number of candidates before a client. If the position appears to be a good match, this could be a good way to find a job because employers using a recruitment agency typically do not post those job openings online.

One of the most effective ways to find a job is networking. How does one network, though, when looking for a first job?

Trade fairs give you a chance to learn about the different companies in the computer device field and make contacts when looking for a job.

Let everyone know you are looking for a software development job. Talk to any contacts you made while interning or working on summer jobs related to the field. Discuss the matter with professionals you made contact with while working on student projects for an industry organization.

Ask your family and neighbors if they know anyone in the industry you can talk to, or if the companies where they work hire software developers. If so, get the contact information for the person and call him or her to schedule a meeting. Another approach is to call a software development manager or director at a company. Let that person know you are a student and would like to get some advice about getting a job in the field. Professionals in the field are frequently willing to talk to students about their career. They may even know of people looking for software developers. If the person you contact does not have a job opening at their company, ask if they know another person in a different organization with possible opportunities.

PREPARING A RÉSUMÉ

Your résumé is the tool that lets potential employers know why they might be interested in hiring you. You want your résumé to get potential employers interested enough to arrange an interview. The résumé includes information on your education, job experience, and skills. When preparing this document, emphasize not only your programming skills but also the "soft" skills that will make you a desirable employee. Soft skills include project management, leadership, and communication skills. The following are some considerations for preparing your résumé.

Use a format that makes it easy to understand. There are all types of trends in résumé styles. For someone looking for a first job, it is best to keep the résumé format simple. Those in this field are very busy. They don't have time to hunt for relevant information. State the type of job you are seeking. If you are applying in response to an advertised job, phrase this section so that it corresponds to the position in the ad. It's simple today to keep a copy of your résumé on your computer and customize it for a particular job and industry. Next, list any full-time, part-time, and internship jobs you've held. Include any relevant volunteer work, such as "taught children at Boys and Girls Club how to program simple games." Finally, list your educational credentials, and any grants, awards, or other special achievements.

Phrase your experience in terms of what you accomplished, not just what you did. In other words, include accomplished goals. "Upgraded software on Little Wanderers Orphanage computer system so that kids would have access to streaming video for preschool learning program," or "Wrote user registration program for computer lab to more efficiently track computer usage." Phrasing your experience in this manner provides employers with the sense that you are focused on accomplishing goals and are aware of issues that companies face.

Don't include a lot of irrelevant personal information in your résumé. However, do include skills or hobbies you know are shared by company management or the person hiring you. If the president of the company to which you are applying is an avid skateboarder and the company has a skateboarding track in the parking lot, you might want to note that you won the Junior X-Games skateboarding championship. List any foreign languages you speak. Also, you should list any charity work you have done because companies today are making an effort to be good corporate citizens and support worthy causes.

When you are done writing your résumé, make sure it looks neat and professional. Proofread your résumé and then have someone else proofread it as well. Make sure you catch all mistakes and typos. Don't rely on a spell checker. It won't catch words that are missing or words that are spelled correctly but are not the word you meant (such as hole for whole). Software development requires precision and attention to detail, so presenting a sloppy résumé could be a deal breaker.

INTERVIEWING FOR A COMPUTER SOFTWARE JOB

The interview is your opportunity to convince a prospective employer that you are the best person for the job. Before you go to an interview, look up information on the company on the Internet. You should go to the interview prepared to explain why you will be an asset to that particular company, given the products they produce. Even if the company atmosphere is informal, at the interview you need to be careful about how you dress. The first thing an interviewer notices is the physical appearance of an applicant. The first step in being successful in an interview is to appear professional. Dress neatly and make sure you are well groomed. Informal doesn't mean sloppy, and sloppiness is a bad characteristic for a software developer.

Be prepared to meet with numerous people, ranging from managers to team members. At the interview software developers will most likely be asked two types of questions, the first being those that are technical. You may be asked about details of

When interviewing for a software development job, it is important to appear confident and professional.

computer programming for the type of application the company makes and about how you would handle a task in a specific language. You are also likely to be asked questions that reveal your people and problem-solving skills. If asked how you would approach a particular problem, remember that the interviewer is not looking for an actual solution to the problem but is trying to get an idea of how you approach problem solving. If you have dealt with a similar problem in the past, mention how you handled that situation. If asked about a skill you don't possess, explain how your general knowledge and experience will allow you to master that skill quickly. You are also likely to be asked general questions designed to reveal your interpersonal skills and how you handle pressure. An example of such a question is, "What is your biggest challenge?" When you are interviewing, be sure to treat everyone you meet respectfully and politely, even team members who you feel are testing you or whose approach to a problem you disagree with. Finally, follow up after the interview by sending a note expressing your appreciation for the interview.

PROFESSIONALISM

Many companies involved in the software industry provide highly informal working environments. However, the fact that the environment is informal doesn't mean that you don't have to act professional. Although you may not wear a suit and tie to work, your clothes should always be neat and clean. You never know when management will have potential customers in the area, and you never know when senior management may be around. Especially in large companies, those in the higher levels of management are more likely to equate competence with a professional appearance. Therefore, they are more likely to promote those who look and act professional in addition to possessing technical skills.

Treat all of your coworkers with respect. This includes support staff, on whom you rely for getting your work done, even if they have annoying traits. Although the software industry has a large number of jobs, in many ways it's a self-contained industry with people moving from company to company as new projects and technologies arise. At a new job, you may well meet someone you worked with in the past, or find that he or she is now working at a company to which you are considering applying.

Also, behave ethically. Do not take credit for others' ideas or work. The more credit you give others, the more cooperation you are likely to get in the future. Keep confidential information secret. Gain a reputation as a person others can trust. This will help you now and in the future.

The types of devices used by consumers are constantly changing. Therefore, the software development field provides great job security as long as you keep your skills current.

Software Development

4 SALARY, BENEFITS, AND ADVANCEMENT

A ccording to the U.S. Bureau of Labor Statistics, there are more than one million software developer jobs, a fact that makes the prospect of getting a job in the field excellent. The bureau states that in 2012 salaries for software developers ranged from $55,190 to $138,800, with a median salary of $93,350. The median salary for applications developers was $90,060, and for systems software developers it was $99,000. Software developers are among the highest paid information technology professionals. Their pay is typically higher than that of other nonmanagerial employees in the computer field. According to the bureau, jobs in software development were projected to grow 22 percent between 2012 and 2022. Given the estimated number of jobs being created during that period, software development offers the prospect of job security and a good salary for a long time to come.

The 2014 salary guide by staffing firm Robert Half, quoted in a *Forbes* article by Susan Adams, disclosed that salaries for employees with skills in the realm of engineering, software development, and programming are growing much faster than average salaries. According to Adams, "At a time when Robert Half projects that salaries will grow, on average, 3.7% in 2014, jobs like mobile applications developer and software developer will see increases of nearly 8%."

PROSPECTS

According to CollegeGrad.com, about 324,000 new computer software engineers are expected to be added to the workforce through 2016. This represents a much higher than average growth in demand compared to the average rate of job growth in the United States. As long as you continue to update your skills, the field carries the prospect for a continued employment. The largest number of jobs, 226,000, will most likely be in the area of applications development; the remaining jobs are expected to be for systems software engineers. The increasing demand for cybersecurity is also likely to contribute to the demand. By 2016 it is projected that more than 1.1 million software developers will be employed. Excellent job prospects are due in part to a rising sophistication in available technology along with the demand among clients for personalized software applications.

BENEFITS

The benefits provided to software developers vary with the size of the company they choose to work for. Large corporations typically offer a menu of benefits equivalent to that provided to other professionals and managers. These benefits often include health, life, and disability insurances; tuition reimbursement; 401(k) retirement programs, usually matching part of the employee's investment; and vacation and sick pay. Companies with large facilities often have on-site cafeterias and exercise facilities.

A company "goes public" by allowing the general public to buy and sell its stock on a stock exchange. When a stock goes public early, employees who own stock can make money.

Medium-sized companies offer a similar range of benefits but may not offer all types of insurance and may or may not offer tuition reimbursement. Some large and medium-sized companies also provide an annual bonus to employees. This bonus may be based on how well the company as a whole does or on the success of a product created by the software group.

Small companies, especially start-ups, generally provide much fewer benefits. However, they may offer software developers stock or stock options, which give the employee the right to buy stock at a reduced price. If the company becomes successful or goes public, which means it begins selling its stock on a stock exchange, this stock can be worth a great deal of money.

PARTICIPATING IN THE SOFTWARE COMMUNITY

The software industry has both formal and informal professional forums where software developers contribute ideas and assist each other and end users. Contributing to the software

Tips for Success

In his article "Skills Employers Want in a Software Developer: My Conversations with Companies Who Hire Programmers," Professor Matt Weisfeld listed the following four recommendations for students seeking a career in software development.

1. Don't get caught up with specific technologies, but focus on the foundational career skills that the employers in this article describe.

2. Rather than focus on the classifieds, get out and network with local programming professionals. I recently read that you are four to five times more likely to get a job through networking than applying to an employment posting.

3. Gain as much practical programming experience as possible through school projects, internships, and self-driven projects. One of the questions that employers are most certainly going to ask you is, "What kinds of applications and websites do you create on your own time—just for fun?"

4. Participate in **hackathons** and other DIY projects. This will not only hone your programming skills but also show that you are passionate about programming.

On BinaryGirl.com, software developer Tamara Cravit of Taylor Software lists the following as the skills required for a software developer.

- The ability to think a problem through methodically and carefully.

Software developers who develop excellent communication, personal, and interpersonal skills are more likely to have successful careers.

- The ability to think on your feet, and to try different solutions to problems.

- Intimate familiarity with whatever development tools you choose to use.

- The ability to write clearly and concisely, and to communicate often technical concepts in a clear, understandable fashion.

- The ability to stay calm and organized under pressure, and to be methodical in tracking your time and setting goals for yourself.

- Enough diplomatic ability to talk to clients, and to explain how to solve their problems, and why the solution you propose is the right one.

- Absolute confidence in your abilities. If you don't believe in yourself and your skills, you can't expect anyone else to either.

community can help you gain recognition and a positive reputation. While you are in college, you can start to contribute to the community by participating in forums on the Internet where users post problems they are having with their software. Some major manufacturers rely on an informal network of "experts" to assist users having problems with their products. Among these are Apple Geniuses and Microsoft MVPs. Assisting others through online resources allows you to get hands-on experience with solving computer problems. In addition, it can give you a chance to make contact with others in the field.

Another way to gain knowledge is to join a professional organization. Two of the largest industry organizations are the ACM and the IEEE. Both have student memberships and special resources for students, including student web pages. Joining such an organization and participating in their activities can give you the chance to work with professionals in the field. These contacts may be able to give you advice when you are looking for an internship or job, or when you are having difficulty with a software problem.

Once you are working in the industry, participating in the meetings and conferences of professional organizations is an excellent way to keep up to date on developments in the field. It also allows you to develop a network of contacts in the industry. Presenting papers at industry conventions and working on committees developing standards for new technologies allows you to help shape the future of the industry. The following are some major software/computer conferences.

- **Interop Conference:** This computer industry technology convention evolved from the COMDEX computer dealers' exhibition convention. It features the latest advancements in the latest computer technologies such as networking, virtualization, cloud, mobility, data centers, and more. It includes two days of pre-conference workshops. (interop.com/newyork/conference)

- **IEEE Conferences and Conventions:** The IEEE sponsors more than 1,400 annual conferences and meetings worldwide, focusing on specific areas of computer and software engineering. (ieee.org/conferences_events/index.html)

- **ACM Conferences and Conventions:** The ACM offers a large number of conferences and meetings each year on specific topics. Some examples include high-performance computing and simulation, software testing and analysis, computer animation, social computing, human computing and learning, and many other topics. (www.acm.org/conferences)

- **Game Developers Conference (GDC):** One of the largest and longest-running game industry conferences for professionals involved in computer game development, this convention features hundreds of lectures, panels, tutorials, and roundtable discussions. (gdconf.com)

- **International Conference on Software Engineering (ICSE):** ICSE is a major software engineering conference for researchers, practitioners, and educators. It focuses on the most recent innovations, trends, experiences, and issues in software engineering. (icse-conferences.org)

MENTORING

One of the most beneficial people you can have in your career is a mentor. A mentor is a person in your field who is willing to provide you with guidance and support. He or she can help you avoid mistakes and give you advice when you have a technical or interpersonal problem. A mentor can be a more experienced developer or manager at your place of work or a fellow member of a professional organization or other contact, such as a person you developed a professional relationship with during an internship. This person should be someone with programming and interpersonal expertise you respect. Ask this person if he or she would be willing to act as your mentor as you start your first

Having a mentor can help one solve problems with technology and people in the workplace.

job. Explain why you chose him or her. Even if that person is too busy to help you, he or she may be able to refer you to someone else. If not, go ahead and seek another person.

If the person you have chosen agrees, stay in touch with him or her. Contact your mentor to discuss the activities you are involved in and any problems you encounter. These may be technical issues that your mentor may have encountered in the past and knows how to resolve. However, you may also encounter interpersonal problems, such as dealing with a difficult team member or manager. Again, your mentor may have some good ideas on how to approach any troubles you experience in the workplace. You can meet face-to-face periodically, such as once a month, or correspond via e-mail.

Even though your mentor is trying to assist you and wants you to succeed, you may not agree with all of his or her ideas. Your mentor can only make suggestions; it is still up to you to decide if the advice is best for your situation. If your mentor's advice is helpful, be sure to let him or her know. Regardless of whether or not you take your mentor's advice, show appreciation for the help offered.

Someday, when you are the highly experienced expert, be sure to take the time to return the favor. Become a mentor to another young developer who is starting out and give him or her the benefit of your experience and knowledge.

KEEPING UP

A software developer's work is never done. Technologies, products, languages, and tools are constantly changing, and competition between companies means that they change rapidly. Software developers need to keep up with these changes in both the short and long term. It's important to stay current with the latest news in technology to gain an idea of what others in the field are doing and what new directions are emerging. In the long term, developers must constantly learn new skills, languages, and tools. Books, trade magazines, and websites provide the means for developers to educate themselves. Colleges and technical schools

Keeping up with new developments in software, applications, and devices is critical to being successful in the field.

Software developers attend a conference presentation. Attending seminars and workshops keeps a developer's skills sharp.

often offer courses in technologies and languages, which can be taken either as a standalone course or as part of a certificate program that requires a few months to a year of study. Certificate programs are also offered in business and can be an excellent way to gain knowledge of management areas such as project, personnel, and financial when advancing into a management position.

Joining and participating in professional organizations such as the IEEE or ACM is also a way to stay current with the industry and learn of new technologies being developed. By working on standards committees in these organizations, developers can even play a role in deciding the details of these new technologies. A career in computer support means a commitment to learning throughout one's career.

ACHIEVING SUCCESS

Achieving success as a software developer requires more than a good education and knowledge of software development.

Those who are most successful truly enjoy working in the field. They have a passion and enthusiasm for creating software and technology. They are willing to put in long hours if necessary. They are able to work alone without supervision and produce high-quality work on time, which is often critical to other parts of the project. Analytical thinking and being capable of breaking a problem down in a logical manner in order to come up with a solution are also important traits. Successful developers have the breadth of vision to see both their part of a project and how all the elements of the project come together in the big picture. Being able to think creatively is also key to success. Having the ability to envision new possibilities and new applications for technologies can lead to new products and solutions to existing problems. Successful developers are flexible. They must be able to adapt to new technologies in an environment that is constantly changing. Curiosity is a valuable trait. People who are curious and learn about everything are more likely to see "relationships" not observed by others. Those relationships may be the key to a new application, product, or technology.

> **"**

> *Design and programming are human activities; forget that and all is lost.*

> BJARNE STROUSTRUP, CREATOR OF THE C++ PROGRAMMING LANGUAGE

Interpersonal skills are also important to success. Brilliant ideas are of little use if they can't be communicated to others, so communication skills are important. To be successful as a team leader or manager, a developer must understand how to motivate people and get them to do their best work. He or she must be able to solve problems with people as well as code. Being a software developer is not easy work, but it can provide a person with a lifelong career that includes the opportunity to be at the forefront of the technologies and devices that change people's lives.

The following are some questions to consider when evaluating whether a career as a software developer is right for you:

- Am I able to get a lot of work done without supervision?
- Am I a good problem solver?
- Am I good at working with other people on projects?
- Can I remain calm under stress?
- Am I a good communicator?
- Do I pay strict attention to detail?
- Am I willing to put in long hours when necessary?

Being a software developer provides the unique opportunity to work on projects that are often challenging, creative, and even fun. At the same time, you are well paid for your work. Whether creating the functionality for new devices, making it possible to simulate events that might occur in the future, or producing new forms of entertainment, being a software developer can be an exciting and fulfilling career. Can you work on your own and manage your time? Do you like math and technology? Are you detail oriented? Can you work and communicate well with team members? Do you want to work on the cutting edge of technology? If so, this could be your chance to play a role in many of the new devices and technologies that will change the way we work, play, and communicate in the future.

GLOSSARY

app store An online retail site that sells applications that can be downloaded to a computer, smartphone, or other electronic device.

artificial intelligence Using computers to perform analysis, processing, and learning in a way that mimics the way human beings think; the intelligence exhibited by machines or software.

avionics The aircraft and aerospace field.

big data Massive amounts of data that require special storage and analytical systems and services.

bug An error in a software program. A bug often stops a program from working or causes it to produce incorrect results.

C, C++, C# A family of computer languages commonly used today to create software.

cloud The collection of servers that store information and data for companies and are accessed remotely over the Internet.

compiling A process used to convert programs written in language people understand to language a computer understands.

computation The performing of mathematical calculations.

GLOSSARY

corporate culture The attitudes, atmosphere, and acceptable behaviors in a company.

customer relationship management system (CRM)
A computerized system that helps sales and marketing personnel find sales leads and cultivate customers.

cryptography The coding and decoding of information.

database A collection of information that can be sorted and analyzed by a user.

data mining The use of computer systems to analyze large amounts of data to find significant relationships.

digital animation Computer-generated images created by using techniques such as 3-D modeling and frame-by-frame 2-D animation.

e-commerce Selling goods over the Internet.

enhance To improve or extend the capabilities of; to increase the worth or value.

enterprise resource planning (ERP) Business process management software that allows an organization to use a system of integrated applications to manage the business and automate many back-office functions related to technology, services, and human resources.

evolve To change over time.

GPS device A device that uses the Geographical Positioning System to locate and provide directions to users. The GPS consists of a number of satellites orbiting Earth that transmit and receive electronic signals.

hackathon An event, usually several days long, in which a group of people engage in computer programming together.

insatiable Impossible to satisfy.

isolate To separate from other elements.

knowledge base A collection of information gathered by experts such as doctors, which can be accessed by users.

lucrative Well paying.

mainframe A large central computer that contains all the software for end users, who access it through terminals that have a monitor and keyboard, but no internal storage.

meteorology The field that studies climate and weather.

GLOSSARY

miniaturization Making objects smaller.

punch card A data card with holes punched in particular positions. The location of the holes encoded the instructions that ran early computers.

robotics The field of designing, building, and programming robots.

semiconductor Pieces of silicon modified to transmit electrical signals. The information to create computer chips is imprinted on a silicon disc, which is cut up to create many computer chips—hence each is a "chip" of silicon.

supercomputer An extremely powerful computer used primarily in scientific applications that require immense amounts of processing power.

wearables Devices that are worn, such as glasses and watches, and perform the functions of a computer.

SOURCE NOTES

INTRODUCTION

(1) pg. 6: Toppi, Hekki et al., "IS 2010 Curriculum Guidelines for Undergraduate Degree Programs in Information Systems," www.acm.org/education/curricula/IS%202010%20ACM%20final.pdf.

(2) pg. 6: Toppi, et al., "IS 2010 Curriculum Guidelines for Under graduate Degrees Programs in Information Systems."

CHAPTER 1

(1) pg. 15: Tsagklis, Ilias. "20 Kick-ass programming quotes," www.javacodegeeks.com/2012/11/20-kick-ass-programming-quotes.html.

(2) pg. 20: Wehle, David, "Robots: The Future of the Oil Industry," www.businessweek.com/articles/2012-08-30/robots-the-future-of-the-oil-industry.

(3) pg. 20: Wehle, "Robots: The Future of the Oil Industry."

(4) pg. 22: Murthy, Sohan, "Women in Software Engineering: The Sobering Stats," talent.linkedin.com/blog/index.php/2014/03/women-in-engineering-the-sobering-stats.

SOURCE NOTES

CHAPTER 2

(1) pg. 30: Weisfeld, Matt, "What Skills Employers Want in a Software Developer: My Conversations with Companies Who Hire Programmers," www.informit.com/articles/article.aspx?p=2156240.

(2) pg. 42: World Wide Web Consortium, "Tim Berners-Lee Biography," www.w3.org/People/Berners-Lee.

(3) pg. 44: BrainyQuote, www.brainyquote.com/quotes/keywords/software.html#yGt4yV804gSRhcT.

CHAPTER 3

(1) pg. 49: Petronzio, Matt, "The 10 Most Profitable Software Companies," mashable.com/2014/04/01/top-software-companies.

(2) pg. 50: Statista, "Number of monthly active Facebook users worldwide from 3rd quarter 2008 to 1st quarter 2014 (in millions)," www.statista.com/statistics/264810/number-of-monthly-active-facebook-users-worldwide.

(3) pg. 50: Oracle Corporation. Oracle Fact Sheet, www.oracle.com/us/corporate/oracle-fact-sheet-079219.pdf.

(4) pg. 52: CA Technologies, www.ca.com/us/about-us/innovation/ca-labs.aspx.

(5) pg. 53: Tsagklis, "20 Kick-ass programming quotes."

(6) pg. 56: Computer Hope, "How do I write my own computer program?" www.computerhope.com/issues/ch000675.htm.

CHAPTER 4

(1) pg. 69: U.S. Bureau of Labor Statistics, "Software Developers," www.bls.gov/ooh/computer-and-information-technology/soft ware-developers.htm.

(2) pg. 70: Adams, Susan, "10 Jobs With the Biggest Projected Salary Gains in 2014," www.forbes.com/sites/susanadams /2013/10/03/the-10-jobs-with-the-biggest-salary-gains-in-2014.

(3) pg. 70: CollegeGrad.com, "Degree Programs for Software Engineers: Online and Campus Schools: Career Information," www.collegegrad.com/careers/proft44.shtml.

(4) pg. 72: Weisfeld, Matt, "What Skills Employers Want in a Software Developer: My Conversations with Companies Who Hire Programmers," www.informit.com/articles/article. aspx?p=2156240.

(5) pg. 73: Cravit, Tamara, "A Day in the Life of ... a Software Developer," www.binarygirl.com/jobs/softwaredev.shtml.

(6) pg. 79: Tsagklis, "20 Kick-ass programming quotes."

FURTHER INFORMATION

BOOKS

Bonnice, Sherry. *Computer Programmer*. Careers with Character. Broomall, PA: Mason Crest, 2013.

Harbour, Jonathan S. *Visual Basic Game Programming for Teens*. Boston, MA: Cengage Learning, 2010.

Miller, Michael. *Absolute Beginner's Guide to Computer Basics*. 5th edition. Indianapolis, IN: Que Publishing/Pearson Technology, 2010.

Staley, Erin. *Career Building Through Creating Mobile Apps*. New York, NY: Rosen Publishing, 2014.

Stent, Amanda, and Phillip Lewis. *The Princess at the Keyboard: Why Girls Should Become Computer Scientists*. Raleigh, NC: Lulu.com, 2009.

WEBSITES

ASEE Student Blog

students.egfi-k12.org

This blog, written by students and sponsored by the American Society for Engineering Education, details key information in the engineering and digital industries.

Career Builder

www.careerbuilder.com

This useful site allows you to search for job openings in a specific industry and city.

GirlDevelopIt

www.girldevelopit.com

A website that provides information about software development classes and how girls, specifically, can get involved.

BIBLIOGRAPHY

Academy of Achievement. "Lawrence J. Ellison." www.achievement. org/autodoc/page/ell0bio-1.

Adams, Susan. "10 Jobs With the Biggest Projected Salary Gains in 2014." *Forbes*, October 3, 2013, www.forbes.com/sites/susanad-ams/2013/10/03/the-10-jobs-with-the-biggest-salary-gains-in-2014.

American Society for Engineering Education Website, www.asee.org.

Association of Computing Machinery. "IS 2010 Curriculum Guide-lines for Undergraduate Degree Programs in Information Systems." www.acm.org/education/curricula/IS%202010%20 ACM%20final.pdf.

Bio.com. "Bill Gates." A&E TV. www.biography.com/#!/people/bill-gates-9307520.

Bio.com. "Jack Dorsey." A&E TV. www.biography.com/#!/people/ jack-dorsey-578280.

Bio.com. "Steve Jobs." A&E TV. www.biography.com/#!/people/ steve-jobs-9354805.

Brookshear, J. Glen. *Computer Science: An Overview*, 11th edition. Reading, MA: Addison-Wesley, 2011.

CareerBuilder.com. "Software Development Jobs." www. careerbuilder.com/jobseeker/jobs/jobresults.aspx?IPath=QH&qb=1&s_rawwords=software+development&s_freeloc=&s_jobtypes=ALL&sc_cmp2=js_findjob_home&FindJobHomeButton=hptest_ignore2.

CollegeGrad.com. "Degree Programs for Software Engineers: Online and Campus Schools: Career Information." www.collegegrad.com/careers/proft44.shtml.

Computer History Museum. "Timeline of Computer History." www.computerhistory.org/timeline.

Computer Hope. "How do I create my own computer program?" www.computerhope.com/issues/ch000675.htm.

Compu-Pedia. "History of Computers." homepages.vvm.com/~jhunt/compupedia/History%20of%20Computers/history_of_computers_1940.htm.

Cravit, Tamara. "A Day in the Life of ... a Software Developer." binarygirl.com/jobs/softwaredev.shtml.

Developer.com. "Three Types of Questions Software Developers Should Expect." www.developer.com/mgmt/three-types-of-interview-questions-software-developers-should-expect.html.

BIBLIOGRAPHY

Economist, The. "Making the Future: How Robots and People Team Up to Manufacture Things in New Ways." April 21, 2012, www.economist.com/node/21552897.

Institute of Electrical and Electronics Engineers. "Scholarships, Grants and Fellowships." www.ieee.org/membership_services/membership/students/awards/index.html.

Linux Information Project. "Linus Torvalds: A Very Brief and Completely Unauthorized Biography." www.linfo.org/linus.html.

Lopp, Michael. *Being Geek.* Sebastopol, CA: O'Reilly Publishing, 2010.

McCoy, Lisa. *Ferguson Career Launcher: Computers and Programming*, New York, NY: Infobase Publishing, 2010

McDowell, Gayle Laakmann. *The Google Résumé: How to Prepare for a Career and Land a Job at Apple, Microsoft, Google, or any Top Tech Company.* Hoboken, NJ: John Wiley & Sons, 2011.

Murashev, Natasha. *How to Learn to Code, Get Your Dream Job, and Change Your Life.* Amazon Digital Services, 2013.

Murthy, Sohan. "Women in Software Engineering: The Sobering Stats." LinkedIn. talent.linkedin.com/blog/index.php/2014/03/women-in-engineering-the-sobering-stats.

Petronzio, Matt. "The 10 Most Profitable Software Companies." Mashable..mashable.com/2014/04/01/top-software-companies.

Pollack, Eileen. "Why Are There Still So Few Women in Science?" *The New York Times Magazine*. October 3, 2013, www.nytimes. com/2013/10/06/magazine/why-are-there-still-so-few-women- in-science.html?_r=0.

Princeton Review. "Career: Software Developer." www.princetonre- view.com/Careers.aspx?cid=145.

Tore, Christopher de la. "New Age of Exploration: Robots Swarm into Land, Sea, and Space." SingularityHub. singularityhub. com/2010/05/06/hold-robot-explorers-to-replace-humans.

U.S. Bureau of Labor Statistics. "Software Developers." *Occupational Outlook Handbook*. www.bls.gov/ooh/computer-and-informa- tion-technology/software-developers.htm.

Wehle, David. "Robots: The Future of the Oil Industry." *Busi- nessWeek*, August 20, 2012, www.businessweek.com/arti- cles/2012-08-30/robots-the-future-of-the-oil-industry.

Weisfeld, Matt. "What Skill Employers Want in a Software Devel- oper: My Conversations with Companies Who Hire Program- mers." InformIt/Pearson, November 12, 2013, www.informit. com/articles/article.aspx?p=2156240.

World Wide Web Consortium. "Tim Berners-Lee." www.w3.org/ People/Berners-Lee/#Bio.

INDEX

Page numbers in **boldface** are illustrations.

ABOUT THE AUTHOR

JERI FREEDMAN has a BA from Harvard University. For fifteen years she worked for high-technology companies involved in cutting-edge technologies, including advanced semiconductors and scientific testing equipment. She was the cofounder of Innovative Applications, a small computer company selling and customizing accounting software. She is the author of more than forty young adult nonfiction books, including *Digital Career Building Through Skinning and Modding*, *Careers in Computer Support*, and *Cyber Citizenship and Cyber Safety: Intellectual Property*.